MY LITTLE
BOOK *of* POEMS

Hardcover ISBN: 979-8-8229-5241-6

Paperback ISBN: 979-8-8229-5242-3

eBook ISBN: 979-8-8229-5243-0

MY LITTLE BOOK *of* POEMS

A.J. Brown

"Faith is not a leap into the dark,

but a step into the light".

Author Unknown

GO ON GIRL

I Say, Go On Girl: To The Afro American Woman, The Jamaican Woman, The Liberated Woman; And, The I'm not going to take this shit anymore woman.

I say: Go on girl, to the woman who takes a back seat to her dreams to make sure her children are off the brow beaten path, and on the right path.

I say: Go on girl, to the woman who has a career and a family.

I Say, Go On Girls: To Our Ancestors who have paved the way for us, and taught these women how to do what they're doing today,

I say: Go on girl, to The Native American Woman, The
The Spanish Woman, The Asian Woman, and The White Woman,

I say: Go on girls, because these women hail from different cultures and nationalities,
They have set an example for all The Go Girls on how to make it in this world today,

We cannot stop here Girls,

We must keep growing, and climbing that ladder to the top,

Then and only then will The Afro American Man, The Native American Man, The Jamaican Man, The Spanish Man, The Asian Man, and The White Man learn to look at us differently,
They will see that we are The Go Girls that make this world what it is today.

GO GIRLS!

BLACK MAN

Black man you say you love me, but you don't come home,

Honey, you don't even call me on the telephone,

You leave my heart in such a fright,

When you don't bother to come home at night,

You say: Baby, I love you and will never cheat,

But you can't keep your eyes to yourself as you walk down the street,

You look at other women as if they were meat to eat,

Everytime I think of all your lies,

I just hold my head and sigh,

You try to tell me nothing is wrong,

But baby I'm tired of hearing that same old song,

When are you going to learn to be true to me,

You need to stop treating me like any 'ole' fish in the sea,

Black man, how long can this go on?
Before you learn to respect me, and stop doing me wrong!

WHERE DO WE GO?

Where do we go when things fall apart?

Who do we turn to when we have a broken heart?

Should we look to our friends for the answer, the key?

Or should we look further to see what we can see?

We should do none of the above,

We should look to our Heavenly Father for Love,

He can give us the directions we need,

Our Heavenly Father is the one to plant that Healing seed,

He's The One that's going to mend that broken heart,

He's the one who is going to put us back together when we fall apart,

When you don't know where to begin,

You turn to your Heavenly Father, Your Friend!

LIVE YOUR LIFE

Life has true meaning for all,

Some people are afraid of not getting up if they fall,

Some people are afraid if they reach out their arms to someone they will fall off,

They sit immobilized, afraid to breathe or cough,

You need to release yourself from fear, or else your life will become miserable year after year,

If you want to live life, and enjoy each day,

Listen to these simple words I have to say,

Be open to life, and don't be afraid,

Don't live your life under a shade,

Learn to love and trust,

If you want to be and feel normal, it's a must,

So don't live your life inside a bubble or cloud,

Loosen up, enjoy life, and be proud!

SUCCESS

Success is not an everyday skill or hobby,

Success doesn't come from the mailbox in your lobby,

You must work hard to become a success,

When you obtain success, you've made it; you're the best,

Success is a thriving need deep inside of you,

It inspires you to be what you want to,

Show the world what you're all about,

Let the one percent know they aren't the only ones with clout,

You have to say to yourself, I won't let anything stand in my way,

Not tomorrow, next year, or any other day,

You must know what you want from life, and plan to get it,

Have a goal in mind, and never quit,

Pick yourself up after a fall,

Go for the gusto, go for it all!

LOVE

Love is something that cannot be explained,

It cannot be held down or detained,

It is a feeling that grows deep inside,

Something you cannot fight or hide,

Love is a deep emotion, some play with it like a toy,

But if you trust Love, it will fill your heart and soul with joy,

If you ever fall in love, you'll know how I feel,

Because the love I have is definitely real,

Infatuation is a totally different thing,

Being in love will make every day seem like the first day of spring,

This emotion Is a gift sent from up above,

There's only one word for it, and its LOVE!

MY DAYDREAM

Each day I go to my sister's place,

I look to see her neighbor's handsome face,

The thought of seeing him makes my day,

I wouldn't have it any other way,

Sometimes I watch him enter his front door,

Then I image us taking a walk along the shore,

We would walk together hand in hand,

Then wiggle our toes in the beautiful sand,

We would sit and watch the sun set,

Then reminisce about when we first met,

In the meantime, I'll be at my sister's place,

Daydreaming about her neighbor with the handsome face.

FEELING FREE

The time has come for me to be on my way,

I'm going to forget the bad memories of yesterday,

I'll be living in the present, and not in the past,

All the good feelings will last,

My mind and body are feeling free,

I'll be living and loving for no one, but me,

I'm going to take my time and do things right,

I'll be feeling free, all day and night,

I'll fight for what's right and question what's wrong,

I'll make my mark on society, and it won't be long,

Life holds a fascination for me,

Doing the right things will keep me feeling free.

LIFE

Life can sometimes be seen as nothing more than a game,

Some people think It's all about who wins, loses or achieves fame,

In the game of life, the stakes can become very high,

But don't give up without a try,

If you combine ambition and common sense, you can make it,

If you don't have any, there's no way to fake it,

Experience and knowledge come by listening and learning,

You won't obtain them by yearning,

Life will always have its ups and downs,

Go for it, try to achieve that golden crown,

Remember, some people will get what they want,

There will be others that don't,

If you think you can do it, you will,

It won't happen by letting your mind stand still.

LOVING YOU

The feelings she had for you were too good to be true,

She had no idea how to love you,

Her feelings were so real, so alive,

She didn't realize you were just talk and jive,

She was so mesmerized, so turned on,

But little did she know, sooner or later she'd be all alone,

Her feelings for you were so strong,

If she had observed the relationship in the beginning, she would of realized it was wrong,

Then she decided loving you wasn't worth the pain she was going through,

It would have been different if you had of loved her too!

THE ENDING

I thought I had you; I thought we had each other,

Our love drifted further and further,

I was lost and didn't want to be found,

The bridge we built, was finally tumbling down,

My dreams of tomorrow went down the drain,

All my hope evolved into pain,

I never knew it would hurt so much,

Once I lost your love and sensitive touch.

GOD'S GIFT

God gave me a gift that's precious to me,

He's my child, and he's sweet as can be,

He's sugar and spice, wrapped up so nice,

He's one of the best things that's ever happened to me,

He makes my heart sing with so much glee,

Because God is with him, he has nothing to fear,

It's like having Christmas 365 days a year,

He's my sunshine on a cloudy day,

He's very special to me, what more can I say!

THE MAY WOMAN

The May Woman has some of the same qualities as a Proverb
31 woman,

She is principled and well-defined,

Always willing to help humankind,

Some women will talk to you about life,

The May Woman will be an example, show you how to handle strife,

Other women will try to tear you down,

The May Woman will build you up, and straighten your crown,

The May Woman will encourage you to be all you can be,

The May Woman will pray with you, and help you fulfill
your destiny,

She will lend you a shoulder to cry on,

Give you words of wisdom to help you stay strong,

She may sometimes seem cool and uncaring,

Trust and believe she is loving, and God fearing,

The May Woman is a sister, friend, mother, and grandmother,

She will love and care for you like no other.

MS. SADIE

Look at Ms. Sadie walking down the street,

She doesn't even have a place to go or food to eat,

Every Sunday morning, she puts on her best,

She wears her big red hat that looks like a bird's nest,

She waves 'hello' to everyone she passes by,

Some people think she's crazy, others just sigh,

She says to anyone that will listen with a great big smile, and a tooth
that glistens:

I am on my way to service you kno,

You'll be lucky if ya see me roun here anymo,

Me and my nest will be going up to that great big castle in the sky,

That's why I'm coming roun here to say my good byes,

People just look and stare,

They act as if they're scared to talk, maybe out of fear,

Next Sunday they look for Ms. Sadie to walk down the street in her
Sunday's best, and her big bird's nest,

One of the neighbors' say: Sadie's done gone by and by,

She made it to her great big castle in the sky.

OUR CHILDREN

Each day I wake up, and ask myself why,

Should I care or even bother to try?

This community is changing into a dangerous place,

I can tell as I look at each child's face,

Some are afraid to attend school,

They are not part of the groups that are considered cool,

Some of the children, and young adults don't have anywhere to live, or anything to eat,

Some of them think life revolves around selling drugs, shooting guns, and hanging out in the street,

Sometimes I ask myself if I am the only one who cares, or wants to try,

Most people today are just shrugging their shoulders, or turning their backs,

It's time for all of us to start picking up the slack,

We need to stop saying: He or she is not my child or children; I don't care,

If we continue to do that, we will be living in constant fear,

If we want our world to be a better place to live,

We must teach our children how to love, and to give,

Show them love and not hate,

This message must be spread from home to school, and state to state,

We must do our part to make this world a better place,

If we don't, there won't be any children left to look in the face!

DIM MY LIGHT

Hey people, y'all need to stay out of my space,

Every time I look around someone's trying to get in my face,

You don't like the way I look, talk, or walk,

Talk to God about it, it's not my fault,

God gave me a light, and He wants it to shine,

Stop trying to criticize me, block, or take what's mine,

Some people can be so negative, even want to fight,

GOD has already said, "You can't DIM MY LIGHT"!

Work on yourself, and get your life right!

ONE WISH

If you had one wish, what would it be,

Would you want to be me?

If you could change something about yourself, what would it be?

Look in the mirror and see,

If you could change your lifestyle, how would you want it to be?

Would you like to start over again?

Would you still want to be my friend?

Or would you rather hang out with rich and famous people?

Be a painter and paint paintings on a church steeple.

Hang out with the homeboys and girls,

Add a bit of street life to your world,

Run through the streets wild and free,

Or maybe recreate history,

Be the first lady to walk on the moon,

Or maybe just sleep until noon,

If I had one wish, it would be,

For everyone to live in peace and harmony!

THE FIRST TIME

The first time I laid eyes on you,

My day changed from cloudy to sky blue,

My heart felt like it was doing somersaults all night,

My brain was saying this is so right,

I kept telling myself: I do not know him well, we just met,

My inner voice said:
What you put into the relationship is what you will get,

I did not want to come on too strong,

I did not want it to end wrong,

I wanted to see if you were feeling what I was,

If you were then, I knew this feeling was love,

I did not want our emotions to fade away too fast,

I wanted this love to last and last,

I started dreaming about our first date together,

The night seemed to last forever,

I had never experienced this type of love before,

I kept thinking about you more and more,

Being together was something we needed to do,

I knew this the first time I laid eyes on you,

It's not just your body I'm after,

I want to share in your joy, pain, and laughter,

What else is there for me to say,

I have waited so long for this day.

THE DREAM TEAM

The Dream Team, that's what we were supposed to be,

Those were your words, the day you laid eyes on me,

Everyone who met us said: What a wonderful couple they are,

Hey, those were just words, the relationship didn't get that far,

Between the arguing and leaving,

There wasn't much room left for believing,

You were too busy accusing me of things I wasn't doing,

But who do you really think you were fooling,

You were lying to yourself, you were lying to me,

The dream team was never going to be,

I'm not sure what dream you had,

What happened stunned me, and made me mad,

The next time you decide to form another dream team,

Make sure you do as you say, and say what you mean,

Your actions and behavior were not of someone who wanted to be
part of a team,

They were the actions of someone suffering from low self-esteem!

FRIENDS OR LOVERS

It started off with a friendly introduction,

Which led to two cups of tea, all the while your beautiful eyes kept looking at me,

The next time we met there was a gentle handshake,

It felt warm and friendly, not fake,

Your voice was so cool and mellow, when you said your heart-warming Hello,

Next came the occasional hugs,

Or was this an expression of your love?

Your mannerisms and disposition let me know you were quite the man,

I knew then it was your heart I wanted to understand,

Our conversations changed from casual to curious,

Will this friendship start to become serious?

Yes, we have feelings for each,

But will we allow them to develop any further?

Friends or Lovers, which one are we?

Which one would you prefer us to be?

YOU

You're brown like cocoa,

Sweet like an ice cream sundae,

Ooh how I would like to kiss you,

You are as bright and sunny as a summer day,

Ooh how I like seeing you,

Your words are so smooth, they flow like a river,

Ooh how I like to hear them,

Your body is so strong, it's solid as a rock,

Ooh how I would like to touch it,

The scent of your cologne engulfs the air,

Ooh how I like smelling it,

When you are near me, there's a chemistry I feel,

Ooh baby I need to find out if you're the real deal!

MY SOUL MATE

Could it be you?

The man I have waited so long to talk to,

The man I have waited to share my life with,

The one to bring me true love, destroy the myth,

Could it be you?

I would be so happy I wouldn't know what to do,

I may kiss the ground,

Thank The Lord, because you've been found,

Make loud noises, and scream with delight,

Go out with you and celebrate all night,

Call all my friends, and let them know,

I've found love, I don't have to look anymore,

I may start to plan that very special day,

I would like for it to be held in May,

I'll start to think about where I want us to live,

Think about all the love we are willing to give,

For now, I'm not sure who he will be,

I'll just have to wait on God and see.

CHAMPAGNE DREAMS

She has champagne dreams and caviar taste,

Today she is eating chicken pot pie, and lean cuisine,

What does it all mean?

She has southern values, mixed with New York style,

Her thoughts are quiet, but she remains agile,

Right now, she is thinking about her future and planning her goals,

The need to make it lies in her soul,

Her champagne dreams and caviar taste will not go to waste.

I CRIED LAST NIGHT

I cried last night, because you and I had a fight,

When I heard the doorbell chime,

I continued to sit there, gazing at the time,

I was thinking about the pain in my heart,

The feelings that kept trying to tear me apart,

The troublesome thoughts that crept into my mind,

The joy I was searching to find,

I cried last night when I heard the telephone ring,

I was hoping the person on the other end would help ease the sting,

The person wanted to talk about their day,

Find out what I had to say,

My thoughts drifted over to you,

I told the person I had something to do,

I cried last night, because I needed us to make things right.

LET GO

Let go, and let love find its way,

Let go, and live for another day,

Let go, and let nature take its course,

Let go, let GOD be your source,

Let go of all the things that could hold you back,

Let go of fiction, and listen to the facts,

Let go of things that make you feel sad,

Let go of people that constantly make you mad,

Let go of emotions that are not real,

Let go of people who don't want to relate to how you feel,

Let go of things and people that inhibit your spirituality,

Even if it means me letting go of you, and you letting go of me.

GOD'S WAY

Following GOD'S ways leads us to the truth, and shows us the light,

Why are some people still putting up a fight?

Why do we sometimes believe in things or people that are not good for us?

Why do we bother to state, "IN GOD WE TRUST"?

Some people are still looking for someone or something to rescue them,

Why not put your Faith and Trust in HIM?

GOD'S ways will never steer you wrong,

You will be encouraged to praise HIM all day long,

Don't put your faith in woman or man,

Turn to GOD because he has the master plan,

Stop allowing yourself to be led astray,

Trusting and believing in GOD is the only way,

"However, as it is written:"

"What no eye has seen,

What no ear has heard,

And what no human mind

has conceived,

The things God has prepared

for those who love Him".

"These are the things God

has revealed to us by

His Spirit".

Corinthians 2: 9-10

A special thank you to everyone that has purchased this book or the audio version of this book!

Peace and Love!

AJ BROWN